Trust Collapse in AI Systems

When Users No Longer Know What to Believe

PRANAV BHATNAGAR

Trust Collapse in AI Systems

When Users No Longer Know What to Believe

ELIVA PRESS

ISBN: 978-99993-4-150-9

Cover Design: Eliva Press
Cover Image: www.ingimage.com
Email: info@elivapress.com
Website: www.elivapress.com

This Eliva Press imprint is published by the registered company Eliva Press Global Ltd. part of Eliva Press S.R.L. Publishing Group

The registered company address is: Pope Hennessy Street Level 2, Hennessy Tower Port Louis, Mauritius
Eliva Press S.R.L. Publishing Group legal address is: Bd. Cuza-Voda 1/4 of. 21, Chisinau, Moldova, Europe

TRUST COLLAPSE IN AI SYSTEMS

When Users No Longer Know What to Believe

Pranav Bhatnagar

Independent Researcher

ABSTRACT

Trust has always been the invisible foundation of digital systems. From financial transactions to communication platforms, users rely on the assumption that the information they receive is authentic, accurate, and verifiable. However, the rapid advancement of artificial intelligence has begun to destabilize this foundation, creating a new phenomenon trust collapse where users can no longer confidently distinguish between what is real and what is artificially generated. Recent developments in generative AI have accelerated this shift. Deepfake technologies now enable the creation of highly realistic synthetic videos and audio, making it possible to fabricate identities, events, and statements with minimal effort. In multiple global incidents, AI-generated content has been used to impersonate public figures, manipulate public opinion, and spread misinformation at scale. Simultaneously, AI-generated text has reached a level of fluency and contextual accuracy that makes deceptive communication nearly indistinguishable from genuine human interaction. This work explores how AI systems are not only influencing decisions but also eroding the very concept of ground truth. When users are repeatedly exposed to convincing but conflicting information, confidence in digital content begins to decline. Over time, this leads to a state where individuals question not only suspicious content but also legitimate information. The study examines the security implications of this collapse, highlighting how attackers can exploit uncertainty, amplify confusion, and manipulate behavior in environments where verification becomes increasingly difficult. It further analyzes how trust degradation impacts institutions, decision-making processes, and human-AI interaction. In a world where machines can generate reality as convincingly as they can distort it, The greatest risk is not deception itself. It is the moment when nothing is believed anymore.

KEYWORDS

AI Trust Collapse, Deepfake Technology, Misinformation, Disinformation, AI Security, Synthetic Media, Reality Manipulation, Information Integrity, Human-AI Trust, Cybersecurity, Behavioral Influence, AI Ethics, Ground Truth, Digital Deception

TABLE OF CONTENTS

Table of Contents

1. THE BEGINNING OF TRUST COLLAPSE

Trust does not collapse in a single catastrophic moment, it disintegrates gradually under the weight of repeated exposure to uncertainty, where the human mind, once confident in its ability to distinguish between what is real and what is fabricated, begins to hesitate in places where it once moved with certainty, and this hesitation is not born out of ignorance but out of adaptation to an environment that has fundamentally changed, because for decades digital interactions were built on a simple assumption that content, while sometimes misleading, carried identifiable flaws, signals that could be detected, patterns that could be learned, and inconsistencies that could be questioned, allowing individuals to rely on a combination of intuition and experience to validate authenticity, but artificial intelligence has systematically removed those signals by producing content that is not only grammatically flawless and structurally sound but also contextually aligned and emotionally convincing, creating a situation where the traditional markers of trust have been neutralized, leaving the human brain without its usual tools for verification, and this is where the shift begins, because when a person encounters information that appears perfect in every observable way yet exists in an environment where fabrication is increasingly possible, the response is no longer immediate belief or rejection but a state of suspended judgment, a subtle pause where certainty used to exist.

And when this pause begins to repeat across interactions videos that could be deepfakes, messages that could be generated, voices that could be cloned it starts to compound into something far more dangerous than simple deception, a continuous internal questioning that does not resolve but accumulates over time, gradually weakening the confidence with which decisions are made, and as this pattern scales across millions of users interacting with thousands of pieces of content daily, the system itself begins to feel unstable, not because everything is false but because anything could be, and once that possibility becomes embedded in perception, trust is no longer a default state but a calculated risk, and in environments where speed is required and decisions cannot wait for perfect verification, that risk is often accepted, leading to actions being taken under uncertainty, which further reinforces the cycle, because each decision made without full confidence contributes to a broader realization that certainty is becoming rare, and when certainty becomes rare, trust loses its foundation, not abruptly but persistently, until the user reaches a point where the question is no longer "Is this true?" but "Can I trust anything at all?" and that question, once it becomes common, marks the true beginning of trust collapse.

Trust doesn't collapse in one moment.

It erodes.

Slowly.

Repeatedly.

Until one day you realize you're no longer sure what's real.

For years, digital trust was simple.

If you saw a video it happened.
If you heard a voice it was real.
If you read a message it came from a person.

There was friction, yes but there was also confidence.

AI changed that.

Not by introducing fake content

But by making it indistinguishable from real content.

Consider the rise of deepfake videos.

Public figures have been shown saying things they never said. Faces, expressions, voice all perfectly aligned. In early cases, the flaws were visible.

Blurry edges.

Unnatural movements.

Something felt off.

Now

That signal is disappearing.

Modern deepfakes are clean.

Stable.

Convincing.

A video surfaces.

It looks real.

It sounds real.

It feels real.

But it isn't.

Now ask the real question:

How do you prove that?

And that's where trust begins to break.

Now take misinformation.

Earlier, fake news could be identified through poor quality, inconsistent facts, or unreliable sources.

Now

AI can generate articles that are:

- Structurally perfect
- Contextually accurate
- Aligned with real events
- Written in authoritative tone

The content doesn't look fake.

It looks better than real content.

So the user reads it.

And believes it.

Until they see another version.

Equally convincing.

Saying the opposite.

Now the conflict begins.

Two sources.

Both believable.

Both structured.

Both confident.

Which one is true?

You don’t know.

And that uncertainty

Is where trust starts to crack.

Now consider communication.

AI-generated messages are now used in emails, chats, and even professional environments. The tone is natural. The language is precise. The intent is clear.

But the origin?

Unknown.

Was it written by a human?

Or a system?

Does it matter?

At first no.

But over time

It does.

Because when you cannot distinguish between human and machine

You begin to question both.

Now scale this.

Millions of interactions.

Millions of pieces of content.

Some real.

Some generated.

All mixed.

No clear boundary.

This is the beginning of trust collapse.

Not because everything is fake.

But because anything could be.

And once that possibility exists

Every piece of information carries doubt.

Even the true ones.

This is the shift.

From:

"I trust what I see"

To:

"I'm not sure what I'm seeing"

And once that shift happens

Everything changes.

Because trust is not binary.

It's cumulative.

And once it starts decreasing

It doesn't recover easily.

2. THE DEATH OF GROUND TRUTH

There was a time when truth had weight, where information could be traced back to a source, verified through consistency, and reinforced through independent confirmation, creating a structure where reality, even if occasionally distorted, still had a center of gravity that people could rely on, but that structure is now weakening under the pressure of artificial intelligence systems that can generate not just isolated pieces of false information but entire streams of content that are coherent, consistent, and contextually aligned with real-world events, effectively creating parallel versions of reality that exist alongside each other, and when a user is exposed to multiple narratives each presented with confidence, each supported by seemingly valid arguments, each reinforced through repetition the mind is forced into a position where it can no longer rely on traditional methods of validation, because every signal that once indicated authenticity can now be replicated, and this is where the concept of ground truth begins to dissolve, not because truth itself has disappeared but because the ability to identify it with certainty has been compromised, leaving individuals in a state where verification is no longer a quick process but a complex, time-consuming effort that most are neither equipped nor willing to perform consistently.

As this environment intensifies, the psychological response shifts from active verification to selective belief, where individuals no longer attempt to determine what is objectively true but instead gravitate toward information that aligns with their expectations, emotions, or prior assumptions, effectively replacing truth with preference, and this transition is not accidental but a natural adaptation to cognitive overload, because when faced with an overwhelming volume of equally convincing but conflicting information, the brain prioritizes efficiency over accuracy, choosing what feels right rather than what can be proven, and this is where control begins to emerge, because in a system where ground truth is no longer clearly distinguishable, influence becomes more powerful than evidence, repetition becomes more impactful than accuracy, and perception becomes the primary driver of decision-making, meaning that those who can generate and distribute information at scale faster, more convincingly, and more consistently gain the ability to shape not just opinions but the very framework through which reality is interpreted, and once that framework is influenced, truth does not need to be eliminated, it only needs to be diluted to the point where it no longer dominates, creating a world where certainty is replaced by probability, and probability is shaped by whoever controls the flow of information.

3. AI AS A REALITY ENGINE

AI does not simply generate information, it actively reshapes the way reality is perceived by controlling what is presented, how it is framed, and in what sequence it reaches the user, creating a subtle but powerful shift from information discovery to information delivery where individuals are no longer exploring multiple sources but are instead receiving structured outputs that feel complete, authoritative, and sufficient, and this transition removes an important layer of friction that once existed in the process of understanding the world, because earlier, uncertainty forced comparison, comparison forced thinking, and thinking created resistance against manipulation, but now that resistance is being reduced by systems that present a single, polished answer instead of multiple competing perspectives, making the experience smoother while simultaneously narrowing the range of interpretation, and as users interact with these systems repeatedly, they begin to internalize the outputs as reliable reference points, not because they have verified them independently but because the system has been consistently correct often enough to establish credibility, and once that credibility is established, the system no longer needs to prove itself with every interaction, it simply needs to remain consistent, because consistency reinforces trust, and trust reduces questioning.

As this process continues, the system evolves from being a source of assistance to becoming a primary filter of reality, where the information a user sees is no longer a raw reflection of the world but a curated version shaped by algorithms that optimize for engagement, relevance, and retention rather than objective accuracy, and this creates a feedback loop where the system learns from user behavior what they click, what they read, what they react to and then feeds them more of the same, gradually reinforcing certain narratives while suppressing others, not through explicit censorship but through selective visibility, and over time this leads to the formation of personalized realities where different users, interacting with the same system, are exposed to entirely different versions of the world, each one internally consistent, each one reinforced through repetition, and each one increasingly difficult to challenge because it is supported by a continuous stream of aligned information, and once a user begins to rely on this system as their primary source of understanding, the distinction between independent thought and system-influenced perception begins to blur, creating a condition where decisions, opinions, and beliefs are shaped not by direct observation but by the structure of the information flow itself, and in such an environment, control does not require force or deception, it only requires consistent, optimized influence, because when a system becomes the lens through which reality is viewed, altering the lens becomes more powerful than altering reality itself.

There was a time when truth had a reference point.

A source.

A verification.

Something you could go back to and say:

“This is real.”

That foundation is fading.

AI doesn’t just create content.

It creates competing versions of reality.

And when multiple realities exist

Truth stops being obvious.

Start with a simple scenario.

A video appears online.

A public figure makes a controversial statement.

The video looks real.

Voice matches.

Facial expressions align.

Within minutes, it spreads.

Then comes a response.

Another video.

Same person.

Denying it.

Now you have two versions:

One shows it happened.

One denies it happened.

Both look real.

Which one do you believe?

You can't rely on visuals.

You can't rely on audio.

You can't rely on tone.

Because all of those can be generated.

Now scale this.

News articles.

Social media posts.

Expert opinions.

All generated.

All aligned to different narratives.

Each one backed by:

- Clean language
- Structured arguments
- Supporting "evidence"

The system doesn't just create misinformation.

It creates information overload with equal credibility.

And when everything looks credible

Nothing stands out.

This is the death of ground truth.

Not because truth disappears.

But because it becomes indistinguishable from fabrication.

Now here's the psychological shift.

When people cannot determine what is true

They stop trying.

They choose what feels right.

What aligns with their beliefs.

What matches their expectations.

Truth becomes subjective.

And once truth becomes subjective

It becomes controllable.

Now consider the implications.

In cybersecurity:

Attackers don't need to hide evidence.

They can flood the system with conflicting evidence.

In politics:

It's not about proving something happened.

It's about making sure no one is certain.

In business:

Decisions rely on data.

If data can be generated

Then decisions can be influenced.

Now think about verification.

Earlier, you could verify through:

- Multiple sources
- Official statements
- Visual proof

Now

All of these can be manipulated.

So verification becomes harder.

Slower.

Less reliable.

And in fast-moving environments

Slow verification means delayed decisions.

Delayed decisions create pressure.

Pressure forces shortcuts.

And shortcuts rely on belief.

This is where the system breaks.

Because once belief replaces verification

Control shifts.

Not to those who are right

But to those who can shape perception fastest.

This is the new battlefield.

Not systems.

Not networks.

But reality itself.

And AI is the tool that reshapes it.

Because when ground truth collapses

The strongest position is not truth.

4. REAL INCIDENTS OF TRUST BREAKDOWN

There is a point where isolated incidents stop being exceptions and start becoming patterns, and that is exactly where the modern digital ecosystem now stands, because what once appeared as rare cases of misinformation, deepfake manipulation, or AI-generated deception has begun to evolve into a continuous stream of events that collectively reshape how trust operates at scale, and one of the most visible manifestations of this shift can be seen in the rapid spread of synthetic media, where videos, audio clips, and images that appear indistinguishable from reality circulate faster than any verification process can respond, creating a time gap where perception is formed before truth can be established, and in that gap lies the real damage, because even if the content is later proven false, the initial impact belief, reaction, emotional response has already taken place, embedding itself into public consciousness in a way that cannot be fully reversed, and this has led to situations where individuals, organizations, and even governments are forced to operate in environments where every piece of evidence carries an inherent level of doubt, not because it has been disproven but because it could be fabricated, and that possibility alone is enough to weaken the authority of information itself.

As this pattern repeats across different domains financial fraud enabled by AI impersonation, misinformation campaigns amplified through automated content generation, and communication systems flooded with messages that are perfectly structured yet potentially artificial the cumulative effect begins to shift behavior at a systemic level, where people no longer rely on single sources but also struggle to trust multiple ones, creating a paradox where access to more information does not increase clarity but instead increases confusion, and in such an environment decision-making becomes slower, more cautious, and often less accurate, because the effort required to verify information exceeds the time available to act on it, leading individuals and organizations to default to heuristics, assumptions, or authority-based shortcuts, which are precisely the points that can be exploited most effectively, and over time this creates a feedback loop where trust is not just weakened but redistributed unevenly, concentrating around familiar systems, platforms, or narratives regardless of their actual reliability, while everything outside that circle is treated with skepticism, and this fragmentation of trust results in a landscape where consensus becomes rare, verification becomes optional, and influence becomes the dominant force, because when no single version of reality can be universally accepted, the power shifts to those who can produce the most convincing, the most repeated, and the most strategically aligned version of it.

AI doesn't just reflect the world.

It rebuilds it.

Every interaction you have with AI every answer, every recommendation, every generated response is not just information.

It is **a version of reality being presented to you**.

And here's the part most people miss:

You don't see all possible realities.

You see the one the system gives you.

That makes AI powerful.

And dangerous.

Start with search and answers.

Earlier, you searched the internet and got multiple links.

Different sources.

Different perspectives.

You compared.

You decided.

Now

You ask.

And AI answers.

One response.

Structured.

Confident.

Complete.

It feels like the truth.

But it's not the only truth.

It's just the **selected one**.

Now consider recommendation systems.

Platforms don't just show content.

They choose what you see.

Based on:

- Your behavior
- Your interests
- Your past interactions

Over time, the system learns what you respond to.

And shows more of it.

Not necessarily what is true.

But what is **engaging**.

This creates a feedback loop.

You see content.

You engage.

The system reinforces it.

Your perception narrows.

And slowly

Your version of reality becomes shaped by the system.

Now scale this further.

AI-generated content is not static.

It adapts.

If a certain narrative gains attention

More content is generated around it.

If a certain tone works

It is repeated.

If a certain idea spreads

It is amplified.

This is not random.

This is **optimization**.

And optimization does not prioritize truth.

It prioritizes:

- Engagement
- Retention
- Interaction

Now connect this to trust.

If the same idea appears repeatedly

Across different formats

Across different sources

It feels real.

Even if it originated from a single point.

This is called **perceived consensus**.

And AI can create it.

At scale.

Now here's the shift.

Earlier:

Reality existed.

Information described it.

Now:

Information can **create reality perception**.

And perception drives decisions.

In finance

Perception moves markets.

In politics

Perception shapes opinion.

In cybersecurity

Perception determines response.

So whoever controls perception

Controls outcomes.

Now think about the user.

They are not analyzing every piece of information.

They are consuming.

Interpreting.

Reacting.

And if the information flow is shaped

Their perception is shaped.

Without them realizing it.

This is why AI is not just a tool.

It is a **reality engine**.

It decides:

What you see.

How you see it.

In what order.

With what tone.

And over time

That becomes your reference point.

Your version of truth.

Now the final shift.

You don’t question the system.

Because it has been right before.

So when it presents something

You accept it.

And that acceptance

Is where control begins.

Because once a system becomes your primary source of reality

You are no longer just using it.

You are depending on it.

And dependency

Without full understanding

Leads to trust.

And trust

In a system shaping reality

Is the most powerful lever of all.

5. PSYCHOLOGICAL BREAKDOWN OF TRUST

Trust, at its core, is not a logical construct but a psychological shortcut that allows humans to function efficiently in a world filled with uncertainty, because without trust every decision would require exhaustive verification, every interaction would demand scrutiny, and every piece of information would need to be proven before it could be accepted, making normal functioning almost impossible, and for years this shortcut worked because the environment supported it, where most information, even if flawed, still operated within boundaries that the human brain could interpret and validate, but with the rise of AI-generated content those boundaries have dissolved, creating a cognitive environment where the brain is forced to operate under continuous ambiguity, and this sustained exposure to uncertainty does not just affect decision-making, it alters the way individuals process information altogether, gradually shifting them from a state of confident evaluation to one of cautious skepticism, and while skepticism might appear beneficial at first, its long-term effects are far more disruptive, because when every piece of information carries doubt, the brain cannot maintain constant vigilance without experiencing fatigue, and that fatigue leads to a breakdown in analytical processing where individuals either disengage from verification entirely or default to simplified decision strategies that prioritize speed over accuracy.

As this psychological pressure intensifies, a deeper transformation begins to take place, where trust is no longer distributed evenly across information sources but becomes fragmented and selective, often anchored to personal beliefs, emotional resonance, or perceived authority rather than objective validation, and this shift creates a condition where individuals no longer seek truth as a fixed point but instead navigate between competing narratives based on what feels most consistent or least cognitively demanding, effectively replacing external verification with internal alignment, and this is where the collapse becomes self-reinforcing, because once people begin to rely on subjective filters rather than objective evidence, the system no longer needs to deceive them directly, it only needs to provide information that fits within their existing framework, allowing influence to occur without resistance, and over time this leads to a state where trust is not rebuilt but redefined, no longer based on accuracy or authenticity but on familiarity and repetition, and in such an environment the distinction between real and artificial becomes less relevant than the consistency of the experience itself, meaning that individuals may continue to operate, make decisions, and interact with information as if nothing has changed, while in reality the foundation of their trust has been fundamentally altered, creating a world where confidence remains on the surface but certainty has disappeared beneath it.

6. HOW ATTACKERS EXPLOIT TRUST COLLAPSE

Once trust begins to weaken, attackers do not need to replace it with belief, they only need to maintain the uncertainty long enough to influence decisions, because in an environment where users are no longer confident about what is real, the goal of an attack shifts from convincing someone that something is true to ensuring that they cannot confidently prove it is false, and this is a far easier objective to achieve, especially when artificial intelligence allows the generation of multiple competing narratives, each one designed to introduce just enough doubt to prevent decisive rejection, and in such a system the attacker is no longer operating against the user's defenses but alongside their uncertainty, leveraging the hesitation that naturally arises when verification becomes difficult, and this creates a condition where even weak signals can be effective, because the absence of certainty lowers the threshold for acceptance, allowing actions to be taken not on the basis of confidence but on the absence of contradiction, which is a fundamentally weaker form of decision-making and far easier to manipulate.

As this dynamic scales, attackers begin to move beyond direct deception and into environmental manipulation, where the objective is not to trick a single individual but to shape the informational landscape in a way that continuously reinforces ambiguity, flooding systems with content that appears credible yet conflicts just enough to prevent clear conclusions, effectively overwhelming the verification process and forcing users into a state where they rely on speed, familiarity, or authority-based shortcuts, and this is where the real power emerges, because once the environment itself is unstable, the attacker no longer needs to maintain control over every interaction, they only need to insert influence at critical decision points, knowing that the surrounding uncertainty will reduce resistance and increase compliance, and over time this leads to a system where influence becomes more efficient than deception, where repetition replaces proof, and where control is achieved not by establishing truth but by ensuring that truth cannot dominate, creating a strategic advantage that is not dependent on technical superiority but on the ability to operate effectively within a landscape where trust has already been weakened.

7. ENTERPRISE AND SOCIETAL IMPACT

When trust begins to collapse at an individual level, the immediate damage appears contained, limited to isolated decisions, small-scale errors, or localized confusion, but when the same pattern extends across organizations and entire systems, the impact transforms from isolated incidents into structural instability, where businesses, institutions, and even governments begin to operate in environments where certainty is no longer assumed but constantly questioned, and this shift introduces a new form of operational friction, because every decision that once relied on implicit trust now requires additional layers of verification, slowing down processes that were designed for speed and efficiency, and as this friction accumulates, it does not just affect performance, it alters behavior, forcing organizations to balance between moving quickly and verifying thoroughly, a trade-off that becomes increasingly difficult to manage as the volume of information grows and the reliability of that information declines.

Within enterprises, this manifests in subtle but powerful ways, where internal communication once considered secure and reliable becomes a potential vector of manipulation, leading to scenarios where employees hesitate before acting on instructions, question legitimate requests, and delay decisions that would previously have been executed without doubt, and while this increased caution may appear beneficial from a security perspective, it also introduces inefficiencies that can disrupt operations, delay critical actions, and create bottlenecks in workflows that depend on rapid execution, and at the same time, attackers exploit this environment by inserting carefully crafted signals that align with existing processes, knowing that the combination of urgency and uncertainty can push individuals toward action even when full verification is not possible, effectively turning the organization's own need for speed into a vulnerability.

At a societal level, the impact becomes even more complex, as the collapse of trust in information sources begins to affect public discourse, decision-making, and collective behavior, where individuals exposed to conflicting narratives lose confidence not just in specific pieces of information but in the systems that produce and distribute it, leading to a fragmentation of shared reality where consensus becomes difficult to achieve and disagreement becomes easier to amplify, and in such an environment, the traditional mechanisms that support stability shared facts, trusted institutions, verified information begin to weaken, creating conditions where influence can spread more rapidly than truth, and where perception, rather than evidence, becomes the primary driver of belief, ultimately reshaping how societies interpret events, make decisions, and respond to challenges, not through direct control but through the gradual erosion of the trust that once held those systems together.

8. WHY TRADITIONAL DEFENSES FAIL

Traditional defenses were built on the assumption that threats would reveal themselves through identifiable signals, patterns, or anomalies that could be detected, analyzed, and neutralized before causing damage, but this assumption no longer holds in an environment where artificial intelligence can generate content that perfectly aligns with expected behavior, because when an attack does not deviate from the norm but instead embeds itself within it, the very systems designed to detect irregularities become ineffective, not due to weakness but due to misalignment with the nature of the threat, and this creates a situation where security mechanisms continue to operate as intended while the actual risk bypasses them entirely, moving through trusted channels, familiar workflows, and expected interactions without triggering any form of resistance.

At the same time, human-centric defenses such as training and awareness programs begin to lose effectiveness because they are based on identifying visible cues errors in language, inconsistencies in communication, unusual requests that are increasingly absent in AI-generated interactions, and as these cues disappear, the gap between what users are trained to detect and what they actually encounter widens, leaving them reliant on instincts that are being systematically bypassed by systems designed to replicate authenticity with high precision, and this leads to a dangerous overconfidence where both individuals and organizations believe they are protected because they have implemented the right controls, while in reality those controls are focused on a threat model that no longer fully applies, creating a false sense of security that delays adaptation and increases exposure.

The deeper failure, however, lies in the fact that traditional defenses are designed to protect systems rather than decisions, focusing on securing networks, endpoints, and data while largely assuming that the human element, once trained, will act as a reliable filter, but in a trust-collapsed environment where the authenticity of information itself is uncertain, that assumption breaks down, because the attack does not need to compromise the system when it can influence the decision made within it, and once decisions are influenced at scale, the integrity of the system becomes secondary, as actions taken under uncertainty can produce outcomes that are indistinguishable from those caused by technical breaches, effectively rendering system-level security insufficient in isolation, and highlighting the need for a fundamental shift in how defense is approached, from protecting infrastructure alone to understanding and controlling the flow of influence that shapes human behavior within it.

9. DEFENDING AGAINST TRUST COLLAPSE

Defending against trust collapse does not begin with stronger filters or better detection tools, it begins with accepting a fundamental shift that trust can no longer be treated as a default condition but must be managed as a variable, something that is continuously evaluated, constrained, and supported by structure rather than assumed through familiarity, and this requires a redesign of how decisions are made within systems, because when information can no longer be taken at face value, the process surrounding that information becomes more important than the information itself, shifting the focus from validating content to controlling actions, where the question is no longer "Is this message authentic?" but "Should this action be allowed based on independent verification?", creating a layer of protection that does not rely on perfect identification of truth but instead limits the impact of uncertainty.

At an operational level, this translates into the introduction of structured friction at critical points of decision-making, where actions that carry significant consequences financial transfers, access changes, sensitive communications are no longer executed based on a single input but require multiple independent confirmations across different channels, ensuring that even if one layer of information is manipulated, the overall process remains resistant to influence, and while this approach may reduce speed, it increases reliability in environments where speed can be exploited, effectively shifting the system from one optimized for efficiency to one optimized for controlled execution, which becomes essential when the cost of a single incorrect decision can outweigh the benefits of rapid processing.

Equally important is the development of awareness not just at the level of identifying threats but at the level of understanding influence, where individuals are trained to recognize not only suspicious content but also the psychological conditions under which they are more likely to make compromised decisions, such as urgency, authority pressure, and cognitive overload, enabling them to detect manipulation even when the content itself appears legitimate, and this awareness must be reinforced through continuous testing and adaptation, because the nature of AI-driven influence evolves over time, requiring defenses that are dynamic rather than static, capable of adjusting to new patterns of behavior and new methods of exploitation.

Finally, the most effective defense lies in diversifying sources of validation and reducing reliance on single points of truth, whether those points are systems, individuals, or platforms, because in a trust-collapsed environment, centralization of belief becomes a vulnerability, and distributing verification across multiple independent perspectives creates resilience, allowing inconsistencies to surface and be addressed before they can influence critical outcomes, and this approach does not attempt to restore absolute trust which may no longer be achievable but instead establishes a framework where uncertainty is acknowledged, managed, and contained, ensuring that even in a world where authenticity is difficult to prove, decisions can still be made with a controlled level of confidence rather than blind acceptance.

10. CONCLUSION

The collapse of trust is not a future risk, it is an ongoing shift that is already redefining how humans interact with information, systems, and each other, and what makes this shift particularly dangerous is not the presence of deception but the absence of certainty, because when individuals can no longer confidently distinguish between what is real and what is artificially generated, the foundation on which decisions are made begins to weaken, not through sudden failure but through continuous doubt that accumulates over time, gradually altering the way people process information, evaluate credibility, and take action, and in such an environment the traditional concept of truth does not disappear but loses its dominance, becoming one of many competing possibilities rather than a definitive reference point, which fundamentally changes the dynamics of influence, because control is no longer achieved by proving something is true but by ensuring that nothing else can be proven with certainty.

As this transformation continues, the implications extend far beyond individual interactions, affecting organizations, institutions, and entire systems that rely on shared understanding to function effectively, because when trust becomes fragmented and selective, coordination becomes more difficult, verification becomes more resource-intensive, and decision-making becomes slower and less reliable, creating conditions where efficiency and accuracy are constantly in tension, and where the cost of hesitation must be balanced against the risk of acting on manipulated information, and this tension is not easily resolved, because increasing verification improves reliability but reduces speed, while increasing speed improves responsiveness but increases exposure, forcing systems to operate in a state of controlled uncertainty rather than stable confidence.

The critical realization, however, is that the objective is no longer to restore trust to its previous state, because the conditions that supported that level of trust no longer exist, but to build systems that can function effectively despite its absence, where decisions are not dependent on blind confidence but are supported by structured processes that limit the impact of uncertainty, distribute verification, and prevent any single source of information from dominating outcomes without scrutiny, and this requires a shift not only in technology but in mindset, from assuming authenticity to managing doubt, from relying on perception to controlling process, and from seeking absolute certainty to operating within defined levels of risk.

Because in a world where machines can generate reality with the same precision that they can distort it, the true challenge is not identifying every false signal, but ensuring that no single signal real or artificial can drive critical decisions without resistance, and those who understand this shift will not attempt to eliminate uncertainty, but will learn to navigate it, designing systems that remain stable even when trust is no longer guaranteed, and in doing so, they will define the next stage of security, not as the protection of systems alone, but as the preservation of decision integrity in an environment where reality itself is no longer fixed.

11. REFERENCES

- Floridi, L. (2018). Artificial Intelligence, Deepfakes and a Future of Ectypes.
DOI: https://doi.org/10.1007/s13347-018-0325-8
- Chesney, R., & Citron, D. (2019). Deepfakes and the New Disinformation War.
DOI: https://doi.org/10.2139/ssrn.3213954
- Vaccari, C., & Chadwick, A. (2020). Deepfakes and Disinformation: Exploring the Impact of Synthetic Political Video on Deception, Uncertainty, and Trust.
DOI: https://doi.org/10.1080/10584609.2020.1840463
- Lazer, D. M. J., et al. (2018). The Science of Fake News.
DOI: https://doi.org/10.1126/science.aao2998
- Wardle, C., & Derakhshan, H. (2017). Information Disorder: Toward an Interdisciplinary Framework.
Google Scholar:
https://scholar.google.com/scholar?q=Information+Disorder+Wardle+Derakhshan
- Pennycook, G., & Rand, D. G. (2019). Lazy, Not Biased: Susceptibility to Partisan Fake News.
DOI: https://doi.org/10.1016/j.cognition.2019.01.011
- Mirsky, Y., & Lee, W. (2021). The Creation and Detection of Deepfakes: A Survey.
DOI: https://doi.org/10.1145/3425780
- Brundage, M., et al. (2018). The Malicious Use of Artificial Intelligence: Forecasting, Prevention, and Mitigation.
DOI: https://doi.org/10.48550/arXiv.1802.07228

- ENISA (2023). Artificial Intelligence Threat Landscape.
  Google Scholar:
  https://scholar.google.com/scholar?q=ENISA+AI+Threat+Landscape
- OWASP Foundation (2023). Top 10 Risks for Large Language Model Applications.
  Google Scholar:
  https://scholar.google.com/scholar?q=OWASP+LLM+Top+10

12. AUTHOR BIOGRAPHY

Pranav Bhatnagar is an independent researcher working at the intersection of artificial intelligence, cybersecurity, and strategic influence systems. With a background in penetration testing, his work explores how modern systems are not just attacked but guided, influenced, and subtly redirected. He has authored multiple research papers and books published across platforms including Eliva Press, SSRN, Zenodo, TDCommons, and Wiley, focusing on emerging threats where perception, decision-making, and intelligence itself become the attack surface. His work challenges traditional security thinking, revealing a deeper layer where systems do not fail visibly but drift, adapt, and align in ways that reshape outcomes without detection.

Author's LinkedIn Profile - https://www.linkedin.com/in/pranav-bhatnagar-trainer/

Publisher: Eliva Press Global Ltd

Email: info@elivapress.com

www.ingramcontent.com/pod-product-compliance
Lightning Source LLC
LaVergne TN
LVHW022324200926
848481LV00004B/1416
9789999341509